CAREERS INSIDE THE WORLD OF

Offices

Office work provides many opportunities.

CAREERS & OPPORTUNITIES

Offices

by Carolyn Simpson

This item was donated to
Spalding University
Book Review Center
through the generosity of

Rosen Pub. Group

THE ROSEN PUBLISHING GROUP, INC.
NEW YORK

ACKNOWLEDGMENTS

Many thanks to the following people for their help in gathering data for this book: Nellie Clarke, formerly of the Maine Teachers Association, Augusta, Maine; Mark Clarke of the State Bureau of Taxation, Augusta, Maine; Betty Jo Bradstreet of Key Bank, Augusta, Maine; Lee Clarke of the Computer Center, Falmouth, Maine; Wendi Clarke, UNUM Life Insurance Company, Portland, Maine; Vickie Hemken of Ponca City Auto Electric Company, Ponca City, Oklahoma; Debbie Shields of Tulsa, Oklahoma; Sharp Temporary Services of Tulsa, Oklahoma, and Carol Smith, of the Job Corps Center of Tulsa, Oklahoma.

Published in 1995 by The Rosen Publishing Group, Inc.
29 East 21st Street, New York, NY 10010

First Edition

Manufactured in the United States of America

Library of Congress Cataloging-in-Publication Data

Simpson, Carolyn.
  Careers inside the world of offices / by Carolyn Simpson.
    p.   cm. — (Careers & opportunities)
  Includes bibliographical references and index.
   ISBN 0-8239-1897-1
    1. Office practice—Vocational guidance—Juvenile literature.
  [1. Office practice—Vocational guidance.   2. Vocational guidance.]
  I. Title.   II. Series.
  HF5547.5.S538   1995
  651.3′023′73—dc20   94-16189
                                                                          CIP
                                                                          AC

Contents

Office jobs range from receptionist to executive assistant.

CHAPTER 1

JOB POSSIBILITIES AND SETTINGS

I thought writing this book would be easy, because I've worked in office jobs. Not only that, I have a lot of friends who have office jobs. But was I in for a surprise! Do you know how many kinds of office jobs there are? You can be anything from a receptionist (who likes to work with people) to a data entry keyer (who might like working alone). You could be a mail clerk (who gets to visit various parts of the building each day) or an executive assistant (whose job it is to make a boss's life run smoothly).

I'll admit I was overwhelmed by all these jobs and the different requirements. So I divided the jobs into general groups to let us take a look at what they have in common and where they exist.

Receptionists

The first group of office workers are the receptionists and information clerks. They greet people, answer telephones, help people fill out forms and find the resources they need, gather information for their employer, and make appointments. Some people (mainly the receptionists) are also expected to soothe the feelings of angry clients.

The receptionists and information clerks work in a variety of settings. Admitting clerks work in hospitals, mental health centers, emergency clinics, and nursing homes. You've met one of these clerks if you've ever been admitted to a hospital. They're the ones who hand you all those forms to fill out. You might see them talking calmly to a patient who's afraid. You might even see them getting coffee for people who are waiting for appointments.

Reservations Clerks

Hotel and reservations clerks work in airports, hotels, and rental car agencies as well as travel agencies. These clerks book your trip, make your reservations at hotels, and reserve your rental car—as well as deal with unhappy customers.

Library Clerks

Library clerks check out books, but they do more than that. They help people find the books as well. Have you ever tried to find a book when the computer was down and you couldn't remember how the Dewey Decimal System worked?

It is essential for a secretary who works in a business such as investment banking, as this woman does, to be organized and efficient.

Financial Clerks
Loan processors and credit authorizers gather information about people's credit history. The data they collect are used by banks to determine if a client gets a loan. These clerks work in banks, other financial institutions, and credit agencies. However, many credit authorizers work in major department stores. They're the people who okay (or refuse) a charge on your credit card if you're over your limit or behind on your bill.

Secretaries
The next group require more specialized skills. They are the secretaries, the data entry keyers, and the computer operators. These people work in state and federal government offices and private businesses. They need computer skills and often business college courses. Although computers may take over many jobs in the future, there will always be a need for good secretaries. Besides typing, word processing, and taking dictation, secretaries have many responsibilities these days. They may screen phone calls for their boss, set up conference calls, and train receptionists. A good secretary is the backbone of most businesses.

Stock and Mail Clerks
Stock clerks and mail-room workers make up another group of office jobs. Stock people take

inventory (counting products bought and sold), store merchandise coming in on trucks, sometimes handle mail orders, and move merchandise to the floor in stores. Mail clerks deliver incoming mail to the various offices and take outgoing mail to the post office. They run the postage meter and sometimes pack mail-order items for shipping. These workers are employed in businesses and stores and in all parts of state and federal government.

Word Processors, File Clerks, and Bookkeepers

Word processors, file clerks, record clerks, and bookkeepers make up the last group. In general, they need to type fast and accurately and have good math and spelling skills. These clerks do a variety of jobs. The better they are, the more responsibilities they have. Word processors naturally spend the greater part of their time typing whatever happens to cross their desk. They and the record clerks may have to locate charts and set them out for the day's appointments. If charts are borrowed, the record clerks keep track of them. They may also be expected to microfilm old records.

Bookkeepers keep track of things bought and sold as well as hours worked and money owed. Payroll clerks and timekeepers fall into this group. You'll find these people (along with billing

File clerks have to be organized. They must be able to pull or put away any information someone needs.

and accounting clerks) in businesses (doctors' offices, hospitals, schools) and state and federal government. The bigger the business or institution, the more specialized the tasks these clerks do. A smaller place might combine the jobs of timekeeper, bookkeeper, and record clerk. Usually, however, timekeepers keep track of employees' work schedules, bookkeepers keep track of expenses and payroll checks, and record clerks find and file the charts.

Questions to Ask Yourself

As you've seen, there are many different kinds of office jobs. The following questions might help you decide which of these jobs appeals to you most. 1) What do office jobs have in common? How do they differ? 2) Which areas of office work are you interested in? 3) Why do you want to work in an office?

CHAPTER 2

ATTITUDES AND SKILLS FOR OFFICE WORK

*M*ary *Ann needed a job when she finished high school. She planned to marry in the fall and wanted to start a family, so college wasn't in the picture.*

After looking through the want ads in the Sunday newspaper, she picked several receptionist jobs and called the numbers listed. Within a couple of weeks, she had landed a receptionist job in a doctor's office. "It'll be great," she told her boyfriend. "All I have to do is answer the phone and do some filing."

But things are not always what they seem. When she got to work the first day, the message light on the phone was flashing.

"Get out some paper and take down all those messages," the office manager told her.

Mary Ann madly wrote down numbers for the nurses to call. But the work didn't stop there. Tired young women kept coming to the counter to check on their appointments. Babies cried in the waiting room.

14 *Toddlers threw blocks at each other.*

Secretaries in doctors' offices generally have a lot of responsibility. This secretary is filling out insurance forms for a patient.

At 10:30 a nurse stuck her head in the door. "Where's the chart on Tommy Shostak? You gave me Thomas Shorey."

"I'll get it. Just a minute," Mary Ann said. But the phone rang again. Mary Ann looked at it and then at the nurse. The phone kept ringing.

"Just hurry up and do something," the nurse said.

Mary Ann picked up the phone. An angry voice shouted, "I got this bill in the mail. How come you charged me so much when I only saw the doctor five minutes?"

Mary Ann looked up at the nurse. "I think you want to talk with the billing department," she said. "Hold on."

"How do I transfer this call?" she cried.

"I already showed you once," the office manager said. "Here, let me do it."

"Will you please get me Shostak's chart," said the nurse. She dropped the other chart on Mary Ann's desk.

Mary Ann looked at her watch. She'd been on the job for only two hours.

Office work can be rewarding. The pay can be good, and the hours regular. But it is not for everyone. You have to have the right attitude, as well as skills, for the job. First, let's look at entry-level jobs. Those are the jobs you can get without any experience or special skills. You might think that anyone could handle an entry-level job. Not so.

For example, some office jobs are very routine. It's fine if you *prefer* to deal with paperwork. Both the work and the hours are predictable. You won't be making life-and-death decisions, but you will be responsible for meeting deadlines, completing tasks, and being well organized.

In some jobs, you sit at a desk in the waiting room in view of everyone who walks in. Naturally, the receptionist needs to like people, first of all, and be able to do several things at once.

Office workers must take a lot of orders, so, of course, you need to be good at following directions. Your boss may give you a list of things to do and expect you to know exactly how to spend the rest of the day.

Skills

Employers will expect you to have certain skills. If you'll be working with numbers, you need to be good in math. If you'll be word processing, it helps to be a good speller or at least make friends with the dictionary.

Some office jobs demand word processing, data entry, or computer skills. You can learn these skills in high school or business school or even on your own. But many businesses prefer to train new employees, so it is important to be able to learn things on the job. Office workers need to be capable and adaptable. Procedures and equipment are always changing. You must be able to learn new tasks or machines.

As with any job, you need to be dependable, loyal, and punctual. You must also be discreet. In some clerical jobs, you may learn sensitive information about people—perhaps even people you know. Don't repeat it to your colleagues or friends. It may end up hurting someone.

A neat appearance and a professional manner are essential if you work in an office.

Personal Traits

If you're going to be using the phone on your job, it helps to have a pleasant telephone voice. You must also speak clearly and loud enough to be heard easily.

Depending on the job, you may need to be friendly and sociable, or orderly and independent. In many cases, you'll need a high school diploma or GED. You do not have to be female to get these office jobs. There are male stock clerks, mail clerks, secretaries, receptionists, and word processors. All you need, male or female, are the right qualities.

Questions to Ask Yourself

Before you decide to pursue office work, you ought to think about whether office work is really right for you. Will you be good at it and enjoy it, or will you regret your decision? Here are some questions to help you find out. 1) What skills are necessary to be a good office worker? 2) What types of attitudes and personalities are beneficial for office workers to have? 3) How do your personality and attitude fit the description you came up with?

CHAPTER 3

HOW TO GET STARTED

*T*wo *young men applied for the same receptionist job. Trevor mentioned on his application having worked two summers as a file clerk in the local hospital, one summer as a volunteer in the library, and two semesters of his high school business course as a clerical intern.*

Don simply noted that he could type and knew a little about computers. "I just graduated from high school, so I don't have any work experience yet," he told his interviewer.

All things being equal, which applicant do you think sounds better prepared for the job? The one with all the work experience, of course.

But how in the world do you get work experience when you're still going to high school?

Volunteering

First of all, work experience doesn't have to be
paid work experience. Volunteer work is just as

A good way to gain experience is by working as an intern.

good. It's what you're learning that counts, not how much money you're making. When volunteering, look for opportunities to learn skills that will be useful in future jobs. Volunteer to help at the library in the summer. Volunteer to be secretary of your church youth group, 4-H Club, or school business club. Better yet, volunteer to work in your school's front office.

People are always grateful for help. And the better the job you do, the better the things they'll have to say about you later when you might need a reference. Look at it this way: You're learning both new skills and responsibility. That's almost as good as money.

Take the time to learn how to use a computer, either at school or at home.
Those skills can only help you to get an office job.

In high school, take as many business courses as you can. If you're not planning on college, you'll want all the training you can get in high school. Don't think that you're wasting your time in school when you could be out in the real world working. Many businesses expect their employees to have a high school diploma. Even if it is not required, they'll probably still choose the applicant who has the diploma or GED.

Entry-Level Jobs

There are several routes to landing your first job. Some people want (or need) a job right out of high school. In that case, you can sign up to take the state or federal exams for government office jobs you would like. The exams are not too hard; you have to show that you can type, spell, read, add, and write. Call your state's Unemployment Office for advice on which tests to take and when you can take them. Tests for entry-level jobs are often given weekly.

After you've taken the test, you'll be put on a list called a "register." When a job comes up, an employer (for the state or federal government) will call you for an interview if you're high enough up on the list. Assuming you make a good impression, you get the job.

If you're interested in working for a private company, check the want ads in the newspaper. However, many jobs are not advertised. Try applying at the personnel department of companies.

Networking

Another way to find a job is to develop some contacts in the community, to build a network. Do you know people at your church who could put in a good word for you at their company? Do your parents know people who could keep an eye out for you at their place of business? It's easier than you think to get people to help you. You just have to make yourself and your needs known and, of course, have a reputation for dependability. This is another way in which volunteer work in your community helps.

Temporaries

Temporary agencies are another way to get jobs. Many people like this approach because they can "try on" a job first. If they find a company they really like, they can try to get a permanent job there. Usually, temporary workers have to complete their contract with the agency (45 working days).

Temporary services are listed in the Yellow Pages. Most of them expect you to call in daily to find out if there's a job for you. The businesses pay the agency; the agency pays you. You may spend a week with one company or only a day, depending on their need. Of course, you have to do good work to keep getting placements. But if you're dependable and adaptable, as well as skilled, you can probably work as much as you like. Clerical workers are always in demand.

Further Training

If you don't need to work right away, you might consider business college, vocational school, or business courses at a community college. The more training and skills you have, the better you'll look to a company.

Before you tell yourself you can't afford to go to college, check out what money is available from the financial aid office. You might qualify for a federal Pell grant, which pays tuition and a small living allowance; a State Regents scholarship, or a fee-waiver scholarship. Some scholarships (which need not be paid back) are based on financial need, and some on academic achievement. If you've done well in high school, you might be eligible. But you'll never know if you don't check it out.

Write for "The Student Guide: Financial Aid from the U.S. Department of Education—Grants, Loans and Work-Study." It's available from the Federal Student Aid Information Center, P.O. Box 84, Washington, DC 20044. Who knows? You might end up with a work-study program. That would give you work experience and a paycheck to boot.

One way to determine what kind of office job you might enjoy is to find work through a temporary agency. That way you can try out several different jobs in a variety of atmospheres.

There's one other route you can take, particularly if you're still of high school age and are having trouble at home. You can find out about a Job Corps placement through your State Unemployment Office. Counselors there can make an application for you. You don't have to have a high school diploma or GED. If you do get into the Job Corps, you can work on your GED there.

You have to show a real need for the training the Job Corps can give you. They look not just at financial need, but also emotional needs. You might be sent to a program in another state. How long you would live away from home in the Job Corps would depend on your training program. The maximum time is two years, unless you go on to advanced training.

In the Job Corps, you're actually an employee of the Department of Labor. You receive room and board and a paycheck every two weeks to cover small needs. Every six months, you can earn transportation money home. There is a system of bonuses for good service. At the end of your program you receive "readjustment money," a lump-sum payment. That way, you can start on a job with money in the bank.

The Job Corps teachers and counselors give you the necessary training and then help you find employment. Some "graduates" of the advanced clerical training program have found clerical jobs (in the transportation field) starting from $6.05 to $10.09 an hour.

Questions to Ask Yourself

There are many ways to prepare yourself for office work. The more experienced you are and the more you know about the job, the more likely you are to get it. 1) What are some methods of acquiring work experience? 2) What courses can you take at school that might help you succeed at an office job? 3) What are some of the different kinds of education available to office workers after high school?

CHAPTER 4

A CLOSER LOOK AT OFFICE JOBS

In this chapter, we'll examine five clerical jobs in greater detail: the receptionist, the secretary, the clerk and clerk/word processor, the book-keeper and accounting clerk, and the credit authorizer.

The Receptionist

Sharon was hired to answer the telephones at a mental health center. She was shown where everyone's office was and where to send clients when they showed up for appointments.

Within a short time, Sharon was the most popular person in the center. Clients would arrive early for appointments so they could visit with Sharon. Sharon was never too busy to listen.

One afternoon, a young woman came in, looking tired and angry. Sharon offered her a cup of coffee and gave her some forms to fill out.

"Well, how am I supposed to fill these things out when I've got a kid to hold?" she said.

Sharon thought a minute. "How about if I hold your little boy so you can drink your coffee. Then we'll worry about filling out the forms. You look like you could use a rest."

The woman gave Sharon a dirty look. "Are you saying I can't handle my own kid?"

"No, I just think you've earned a break," Sharon said. "And besides, I love kids. Look, I have some crayons in my desk. He can color, and you can relax a little. I promise you can have him back."

Before the woman could say anything, the little boy had followed Sharon to her desk. The woman leaned back in her chair, sipped some coffee, and closed her eyes. The others in the waiting room smiled and went back to reading their magazines.

Salary Range: $10,000 to $18,000 a year, depending on your experience and where you work.

Description of Job and Skills

Receptionists are usually the first people you meet when you enter an office. They are the ones who greet you and let you know you've come to the right place (or not). They're the ones who hand you all those forms to fill out.

Receptionists are the ones who answer the phones, too. Some wear a headset, which lets

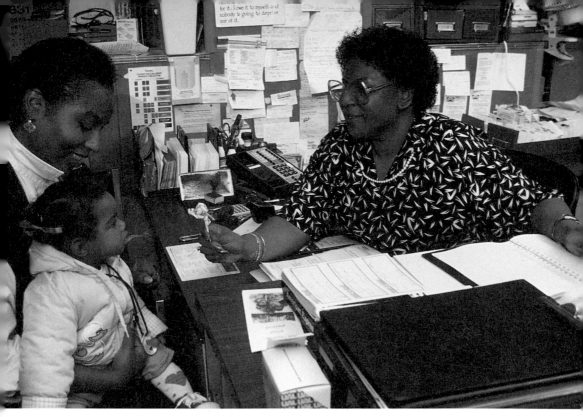

A pleasant personality helps create a welcoming atmosphere in an office.

them answer the phone while they type and do other things. Some work a switchboard. Receptionists usually need to be able to do light word processing and know (or learn) how to use other kinds of programs on a computer. Many company reports are stored on computer these days. Some receptionists file records, sort mail, and serve coffee to visitors. In some places, receptionists even act as security, keeping out people who don't belong in the building.

To be a receptionist, you need a pleasant voice. If you sound tired or angry, you won't make a very good impression on people.

Secretaries today do more than just type, answer phones, and take dictation. This man is preparing a statistical report.

Receptionists usually need to know how to run a few office machines. You may be expected to type and make photocopies, too. If you don't have good typing skills, at least be willing to learn. It helps if you can spell and have neat, clear handwriting.

Receptionists need to be able to handle all kinds of situations: the patient who brings her toddlers to her appointment, the guy who's angry about his bill, or the couple who start fighting in public. Working so closely with the public, receptionists need to like people. They must be dependable and responsible. When you're in charge of the front office, you can't arrive late, forget important messages, or be unorganized.

The Good Points

The work has plenty of variety.

Job opportunities are plentiful. Some office jobs are being taken over by computers, but there will always remain a need for real people as receptionists.

You'll meet a variety of new and familiar faces. You can be helpful without having to feel totally responsible for their needs.

With training, you have the chance to advance in your company.

You can often find these jobs through temporary agencies.

Receptionists are not often laid off. A company might have to lay off its middle managers or even its maintenance staff, but you can't run a business without the people out front.

Finally, a receptionist position is a good entry-level job, with predictable, regular hours.

The Bad Points

The pay is not as high as jobs requiring more skills.

Some people get frustrated having to do too many things at once. You don't have much privacy.

When you're sitting out front, you're usually the first person to see trouble coming. In a society that's seeing more violence on the job, being out front can be a problem.

The Secretary

John had a million things to do when he got to the office. His boss had asked him to send a memo to the staff about the new dress code. She hadn't written the memo; she expected John to write it himself.

A few minutes later, a new employee stopped by to talk to John's boss.

"She's in a meeting right now," John said. "Why don't you call me back in an hour?"

"Just give me her extension, and I'll call her in an hour," the man said.

"I take her calls," John said. "Call me, and I'll transfer the call."

"How come you get her calls? You surely don't screen all her inside calls. We all work together."

"Well, that's how it works," John said. "She's a busy person, and I have to see that she isn't interrupted unless it's necessary. That's my job."

Salary: $21,000 to $33,000 a year

Description of Job and Skills

Today's secretary does a lot more than type, take dictation, and answer the phone. Nowadays, he or she arranges conference calls, does research, prepares statistical reports, and sometimes answers correspondence on his own. He answers the phone and decides which calls his boss needs to take and which can wait. He runs the office equipment (or has his clerical staff do it), takes dictation, and arranges meetings.

All these different tasks are done to make his boss's life run smoothly. That's what his job boils down to. In fact, that's why many are called administrative assistants rather than secretaries.

The secretary needs the same qualities as the receptionist. He or she needs to know how to dress correctly and talk politely (but firmly, if necessary).

However, he needs more specialized skills. He must be competent using a word processor or computer and have excellent shorthand and typing skills.

Secretarial jobs are not usually entry-level positions. They often require some work experience.

Because he represents his boss, he must have excellent communication skills. And any good secretary must be dependable, loyal, and responsible. Good secretaries are in demand, but a lot of people have the skills. Further education (either from a community college or business college) often helps an applicant stand out and get the job.

The Good Points

The job is well paid, and there are many opportunities to advance in a company.

As an administrative assistant, you always have

access to the boss.

You deal with more challenges than the clerk/ word processor does. You have more responsibilities and some leeway to act on your own.

Usually, as you move up in responsibilities and pay, you'll see a better benefit package as well.

And finally, the hours can be regular and predictable.

The Bad Points

This is not usually an entry-level position. You'll probably need some related work experience before being considered for the job. You may also need some college courses.

Your boss may expect you to handle personal matters like picking out gifts for family members, or meeting her at the airport. Your boss may want you to keep people out of her hair at times, and that means being firm with others (which may not be your style).

Finally, you may be expected to stay late and come to work on short notice.

The Clerk and Clerk/Word Processor

Sylvia took a job as a clerk/word processor with a major airline company when she graduated from high school. She had only taken a job to earn some money so she could get her own apartment. But as the months passed and her skills and reliability got noticed, she thought about moving up in the company. Two years later, Sylvia became assistant supervisor of her department. When her boss retired the following year, Sylvia was made department head.

"I'm going to take some business courses at the community college," Sylvia told her mother one evening. "I'd like to try my hand in management."

Within three years, Sylvia had her Associate's Degree in Business Management, having attended college in the evenings and on weekends. Five years later, Sylvia became a vice president of the company.

Office jobs can be a good start to other careers.

Salary: $14,000 to $22,000 a year, depending on the city and whether you work for the government or a private business.

Description of Job and Skills

The clerk (record clerk or file clerk) spends a good part of the day pulling charts, making entries in them, and putting them back. He or she probably uses office equipment such as a fax machine, typewriter or word processor, dictation machine, photocopier, and microfilmer.

A clerk might also have to proofread reports, sort mail, and stuff envelopes. She might copy data from one report to another.

Most of these tasks are routine, so you need to like routine. You also need to be dependable and a steady worker. Often you'll be left to take care of your day's work with little supervision.

Of course, you need good word processing

Clerks and word processors usually work independently.

skills. Most employers test applicants and usually hire those with the best skills.

Beyond that, you need to know how to spell (or at least use a dictionary) and how to add.

Some clerks are hired without a lot of skills, as long as they are willing to learn on the job. So it helps to be willing to learn.

You also need to be discreet. Typing reports (especially from health records) gives you all kinds of personal information. It is unprofessional to share that knowledge.

The Good Points

These jobs have predictable routines and regular hours. You won't get many surprises.

As a clerk, you must be able to set and meet your own deadlines and goals.

You usually won't have to mingle with the public unless you're filling several different roles in a company. Clerks and clerk/word processors are usually left to do their own thing.

You may have a variety of tasks and the opportunity to tackle them in the order you want.

These are entry-level jobs. You don't necessarily need much experience or a college degree, but you can move on to other jobs. In fact, because so many people move on from these jobs, new positions are always opening up.

The pay is lower, but the job responsibilities are less than in some office jobs. Temporary agencies use a lot of clerks and clerk/word processors.

With time and good performance, you can end up heading your department.

The Bad Points

Because you are on your own most of the time, you might feel isolated or lonely.

It is a very predictable job.

The salary is low in this type of entry-level job.

There may be fewer of these jobs in the future because computers can do much of the work.

Finally, you must be able to set your own goals and meet deadlines because it will be up to you to complete your work. No one will stand over you to make you do it.

The Bookkeeper and Accounting Clerk

Adam was hospitalized with appendicitis. While he recovered, his phone never stopped ringing. People kept calling to wish him well, and to beg him to come back to work.

A traveling salesman for the company Adam worked for called. "Adam," he said. "You always took care of my expense checks on time. I really miss you now."

Another woman called. "Adam," she said, "when I wasn't sure I had enough leave time to take that vacation, you worked late trying to find any errors. I really miss you now."

His boss called several times. "I can't tell if we're making a profit anymore or not. The bills are piling up, and, well, I really miss you now."

Adam hadn't realized what an important job he'd been doing for the company. Sure, he took care of everyone's expense checks, seeing that they got written up and signed. Sure, he updated the inventory in the computers, kept track of people's leave requests, and paid the bills. But was that such a big deal? he thought.

A balloon bouquet arrived, with a note attached. "Get well soon," it read. "We can't run this place without you."

Salary: $12,000 to $22,000 a year, depending on the size of the business and your years of experience.

Description of Job and Skills

Bookkeepers' tasks differ depending on the nature of the business. Most bookkeepers are expected to handle the invoices and the monthly bank statements and balance the books. They may prepare payroll and travel checks for signing. They may have to enter data into computers for storage, and sometimes do inventory work. If they work in a store, they may have to check packing slips and input new prices on product lines.

A bookkeeper or accounting clerk needs a good head for numbers. The bookkeeper needs some typing skills, filing ability, knowledge of a ten-key calculating machine, and a general knowledge of computers. It's helpful to have a general knowledge of accounting principles. If you're interested in an accounting position, it makes sense to get extra training in accounting (beyond high school business courses).

Both the bookkeeper and accounting clerk need to have "diplomatic" skill. When you talk to people about money, you need to be tactful but at the same time able to stand up for yourself. People often question their paychecks; you can't just yell back at them, even if you think you're right.

You will probably be dealing with the public at times, so you will need a pleasant telephone voice.

Depending on the size of your company and your experience, you have
the potential to advance in responsibility and earn more money.

You must be discreet. No one needs to know
how well your company is (or isn't) doing or how
much any staff member may make. Employees
want to believe you're able to keep secrets.
Especially theirs.

The Good Points

Depending on the size of your company and your
experience, you have the potential to earn good
money.

You'll have clearly defined tasks, and usually
the authority to carry them out, which means
you'll have much responsibility.

In some cases, you may not have to deal with

the public. Your hours will be regular and the benefits good.

As in other office jobs, if you're dependable and your performance is good, you can move up to a supervisory position.

The Bad Points

Job opportunities are decreasing because computers are taking over many bookkeeping tasks.

If you can't work independently (or don't believe in yourself), you won't like this job. It can become a hassle if you make a mistake, like letting the paychecks be late, that affects your fellow employees.

The Credit Authorizer

Nadine worked in a large department store. She always looked forward to the holidays, despite the extra hours of work. After all, she was needed more to settle problems that cropped up with holiday shoppers.

On this day a clerk called to say that a Code 4 had shown on a customer's charge. Code 4 meant the person was over the credit limit. Nadine looked up the woman's account on the computer; it was already over by $50. "How much is she charging?" she asked the clerk.

"$43.52," the clerk said.

"Okay, let her charge it. It's Christmas."

Nadine put the phone down. She always felt good when she okayed a charge.

A few minutes later, the phone rang again. Another customer wanted to charge over her limit, but this time Nadine saw that the account hadn't been paid that month. "How much does she want to charge?" she asked.

"$123.75," the clerk said.

"Oh, that's a little high," Nadine said. "Let me talk with the customer."

The clerk handed the phone to the customer, who sounded nervous. "What's the problem?" she said.

"Well, you're over your limit, for one thing," Nadine said.

"It's Christmas; everybody goes over their limit," the woman said.

"Yes, but you haven't made a payment this month," Nadine said.

"Well, I've always been on time before. I don't see that this is a problem. You want my business, don't you?" The woman was sounding angry.

Nadine didn't like arguing with a customer over the phone. "Why don't you come up to the office, and we can talk about it," she suggested.

Putting the phone down, she looked at the other woman in the office. "It's such a challenge trying to keep the customer and the store happy at the same time!"

Salary: $12,800 to $19,850 a year.

To be a credit authorizer you need good communication skills.

Description of Job and Skills

Credit authorizers review information on retail credit applications and check into any problems they spot. Of course, they do not approve loans, but department store credit authorizers may approve store credit cards.

Other credit authorizers gather information for credit forms and talk with other credit bureaus. They communicate their decisions to the agencies or banks that use them.

Those who work in stores decide whether or not a customer can charge more on his or her credit card. If a problem develops, they handle it.

47

Some credit authorizers prepare papers for real estate settlements, but they do not decide whether the loan is approved.

To be a credit authorizer you need good communication skills (including a good telephone voice). You need an eye for detail (to spot problems), diligence (to follow up on information), and confidence (to handle angry customers).

Like other clerks who know a lot of personal information, you must be discreet. You can't talk about what you know.

You may need PC keyboarding experience and typing skills, as well as good math and spelling skills.

The Good Points

These jobs can lead to better-paying jobs, particularly if you get more training.

They involve both working with people and being on your own. You have the best of both worlds: responsibility and independence, but not too much of either.

The work is not boring. The hours are usually predictable and regular (unless you're working in a department store).

This is an entry-level job. You can pick up what skills you don't have through in-house training programs.

The Bad Points

If you don't like working with numbers or tracking down information, you won't like this.

You need to be able to work with little or no supervision.

The tasks can become repetitious, and you don't have any real authority.

You may have to work overtime if you work in a department store during the holiday season. In real estate, the busy times are spring and summer and the end of the month.

Questions to Ask Yourself

Now that you've learned about all the different types of clerical jobs, you need to decide if any of them appeal to you, and if so, which. 1) What are some of the responsibilities of a person in a clerical position? 2) Do you like working with people or alone? 3) What skills does a clerical worker need?

CHAPTER 5

TIPS FOR GETTING THE JOB AND KEEPING IT

Now that you're prepared for a job hunt, let's look at how to write a résumé, so you'll be prepared for that first interview. You'll want to put yourself on paper in the best possible light.

The Résumé

Start your résumé with your name, address, and phone number. Include a section on your education and work experience. Even if you haven't gone to college, be sure to note that you have your high school diploma or GED.

Under work experience, be sure to mention any volunteer work you've done. If you worked two summers at the library, put it down, as well as what you did there. If you held office in a school or church group, mention it; it tells employers that you've handled responsibilities.

Always work from your current job back. If you

held a lot of jobs for short periods of time, just mention the jobs, not the dates.

Type your résumé, particularly if you're looking for typing work. Check for spelling errors.

If you're still not sure exactly what to put in your résumé, check out a book on résumé writing. You can find them in the library as well as most bookstores.

Some businesses test not only your typing, math, and spelling skills, but your writing as well. Be prepared to do a writing sample when you're interviewed.

The Interview

This is where the employer gets an idea of your abilities. If you'll be working with the public, he or she will also be concerned about the impression you make.

Here are some tips to help you make the best possible impression. First of all, dress appropriately. Wear conservative clothes that are clean and pressed. Check the mirror before you walk out of your house. What does it say about you?

Never be late for an appointment! In fact, it's a good idea to arrive ten to fifteen minutes early. Most employers will want you to fill out an application, even if you have your résumé with you.

Practicing

The night before the interview, try to think what

This young woman is taking part in a job training program at her high school in Brooklyn, New York. She is learning the dos and don'ts of interviewing.

you might be asked and practice your answers. Most employers will want to know what you think are your strengths and even your weaknesses. It is not bragging to mention some strengths, such as dependability, skill, or independence.

If you have to come up with a "weakness," make sure you pick one that is really a strength. "Well, I tend to work too hard" or "I'm a perfectionist" sound like weaknesses, but neither really is. There's nothing a employer likes to hear better than that an employee works hard.

Even if you've practiced your answers for three

Brush up on all your skills before an interview. You want to be able to give your top performance if you are asked to take a typing or other kind of test.

days straight, don't let it show. Make it sound as if you just thought them up.

A Few Don'ts

Never badmouth any previous employer. Even if she was a first-class jerk, don't let on.

Keep nervous habits at bay. Don't bite your nails (even if you do it at home). Don't twist your hair around your fingers. Don't tap your pen on the desk. Don't jiggle your foot. Don't throw "you know" and "like" into every sentence.

Don't ask what the pay is in the first three minutes of the interview. Leave salary and benefits for later.

Some Dos

Show an interest in the company or the job, but don't overdo it. Most people can tell when you're exaggerating.

Be sure you catch the name of the interviewer. Use it during the conversation, and write it down to be sure of the spelling. People like being addressed by name. As you leave, thank the interviewer. Follow up with a thank-you note within the week. Your note will be a reminder of your interview and show that you have manners.

If you haven't heard anything after a week (unless they say wait two weeks), call for an update. Be polite. You want to show persistence, not aggression, in your job hunt.

If you follow these tips, you'll get a job sooner

or later. And now for some tips on how to keep
that job.

Keeping the Job

First of all, be dependable. Show up every day on
time and ready to work.

Stick to the time limits of your breaks. Don't
try to squeeze in extra time because you're not
really busy. Those things get noticed.

Dress appropriatcly. Most offices have a dress
code. Be sure to follow it.

Above all, be discreet. Don't sit around
gossiping. Even looking as if you're gossiping
makes you look bad.

Don't show up with a hangover. Don't try to
challenge the smoking rules.

Don't abuse sick leave. You may need a week's
leave someday, and if you eat away at the time
now, you won't have it later.

Finally, don't complain about your boss to
everyone who comes within earshot. If you have a
gripe with your boss, take it up with him or her.
Be polite and listen to the other side. Maybe
there's room to compromise. If the boss is
unbearable to work with, transfer out of the
department or look for another job. Better to
do that than whine and feel miserable.

Sexual Harassment

You may run into the problem of sexual harassment.
Sexual harassment can include someone pressuring

Once you have the job, you must live up to your responsibilities.

Remember that there is usually the potential for advancement. This executive is the head of her office.

you to go out with him or her and telling dirty jokes that make you feel uncomfortable on the job. Some states consider anything that intimidates a person on the job to be a form of harassment, whether the boss or a coworker does it. If you have a valid complaint, ask the Human Resources Department of your company for a copy of their sexual harassment guidelines. They will tell you how to file a grievance. It's against the law to harass a worker.

If you're a dependable worker and willing to learn new skills as you go along, you'll have a long career inside the world of offices. Not only

You might even end up owning your company. Laurie Jones and her husband started Jones Technologies Inc., a company that provides customer service for computer companies.

that; you'll probably get promoted along the way. You'd be surprised at the number of businessmen and women who began in entry-level office jobs.

Questions to Ask Yourself

It's always a good idea for you to get a head start on preparing for a job. 1) What information would you include on your résumé? 2) How should you dress for an interview? 3) What are some questions you might ask a potential employer?

SELF-EVALUATION TEST

On a separate sheet of paper answer the following questions as honestly as possible. There are no right or wrong answers. When you've completed each section, read the comments that follow.

1. Do I like working around people?

2. Can I handle more than one task at a time?

3. Do I have a pleasant telephone voice?

4. Can I type accurately, print well, and spell correctly?

5. If I can't spell, am I willing to look words up in a dictionary?

6. Can I be counted on to be on time?

7. Can I handle a job with little direct supervision?

8. Can I handle angry clients or customers without losing my cool?

9. Can I keep my personal life separate from my job?

10. Can I be counted on to remain calm in an emergency or "unusual" situation?

If you answered yes to most of the above questions, you might like the positions of receptionist, secretary, admitting clerk, or information clerk.

1. Do I prefer working independently?

2. Am I willing to seek additional training?

3. Do I like repetitive kinds of activities?

4. Can I be discreet with information?

5. Can I be counted on to be on time and not to overstay my breaks even if no one is watching me?

6. Do I have good skills in typing, data entry, math, and grammar?

7. Do I prefer working with figures and graphs to working with people?

8. Am I good at detail?

9. Can I handle angry customers?

If you answered yes to most of these questions, you might like credit authorizer positions, bookkeeping and accounting positions, record clerk positions, data entry keyer, filing, and typing positions. These jobs require less contact with the public and more repetitive work.

If you like frequent changes in scenery and tasks, as well as not having to dress up, you might look into stock clerk and mail clerk positions.

GLOSSARY

applicant Person applying for a job.

Associate's Degree Two-year college degree.

communication skills Speaking and writing skills.

community college Formerly called "junior college," two-year college that offers an Associate's Degree.

conference call Three or more people at different locations on one phone call.

electronic filing Filing records in a computer; adding to and changing the data.

entry-level position Job that requires no previous work experience.

flexible hours Work hours arranged around people's different needs.

in-house training Training on the job.

microfilming Storing records on film that can later be read with a microfilm viewer.

reference Recommendation for a job from someone who knows you.

repetitious Done over and over again.

switchboard Telephone system that is manned by an operator (often the receptionist), who routes the calls to the right extensions.

temporary agency Employment agency for temporary jobs.

FOR FURTHER READING

Berger, Melvin. *Word Processing*. New York: Franklin Watts, 1984.

Czukor, John. *Beginning Office Worker*. New York: Arco, 1988.

Doyle, Jean Monty, and Dennis, Robert Lee. *The Complete Handbook for Medical Secretaries and Assistants*. Boston: Little, Brown, 1978.

Fry, Ron. *Your First Job*. Hawthorne, NJ: Career Press, 1993.

Jaderstrom, Susan; Kruk, Leonard; and Miller, Joanne. *Professional Secretaries International Complete Office Handbook*. New York: Professional Secretaries International, 1992.

Kennedy, Marilyn Moats. *Glamour Guide to Office Smarts*. New York: Fawcett Columbine, 1986.

Lewis, William, and Schuman, Nancy. *The Temp Worker's Handbook*. New York: AMACOM, 1988.

Occupational Outlook Handbook, 1992–1993. Washington, DC: U.S. Department of Labor, Bureau of Labor Statistics.

Pedersen, Laura. *Street-Smart Career Guide*. New York: Crown Trade Paperbacks, 1993.

Petras, Kathryn and Ross. *Jobs '93*. New York: Simon and Schuster, 1993.

INDEX

About the Author

Carolyn Simpson has worked as a social worker in both Maine and Oklahoma. She currently teaches psychology at Tulsa Junior College and lives on the outskirts of Tulsa with her husband and their three children.

Cover Photo: Image Bank © Benn Mitchell
Photo Credits: Impact Visuals pp. ii, 9, 47, 56 © Hazel Hankin, p. 12 © Ansell Horn, p. 2, 39 © George Cohen, pp. 12, 44 © Martha Tabor, p. 36 © Rick Gerharter, p. 40 © Earl Dotter, p. 52 © Cindy Reiman, p. 53 © Dirk Condyles, p. 57 © Loren Santow; Image Bank p. 18 © Brett Froomer, pp. 21, 31 © Kay Chernush, p. 22 © Maria Taglienti, p. 26 © Janeart Ltd., p. 32 © Theodore Anderson; all other photos © AP/Wide World Photos
Photo Research: Vera Ahmadzadeh with Jennifer Croft
Design: Kim Sonsky